50 Decadent Strawberry Cake Layer Recipes

By: Kelly Johnson

Table of Contents

- Classic Strawberry Shortcake Layer Cake
- Strawberries and Cream Drip Cake
- Strawberry Cheesecake Layer Cake
- Chocolate-Dipped Strawberry Cake
- Strawberry Velvet Cake
- Strawberries and Chantilly Cream Cake
- Strawberry Lemon Layer Cake
- White Chocolate Strawberry Cake
- Strawberry Mousse Layer Cake
- Strawberry Mascarpone Layer Cake
- Fresh Strawberry Buttercream Cake
- Strawberry Almond Cake
- Strawberry-Basil Layer Cake
- Strawberry-Raspberry Layer Cake
- Strawberry Coconut Cream Cake
- Strawberry Lime Margarita Cake
- Strawberry Rosewater Cake
- Strawberry Oreo Layer Cake
- Triple Strawberry Delight Cake
- Strawberry Brownie Cake
- Strawberry Cream Cheese Pound Cake
- Strawberry Funfetti Celebration Cake
- Strawberry Matcha Layer Cake
- Strawberry Tiramisu Cake
- Strawberry Vanilla Bean Cake
- Dark Chocolate Strawberry Truffle Cake
- Strawberries and Caramel Layer Cake
- Strawberry Mint Layer Cake
- Strawberry Angel Food Layer Cake
- Roasted Strawberry and Honey Cake
- Strawberry and Pistachio Layer Cake
- Strawberry Cream Mille Crepe Cake
- Strawberry Champagne Cake
- Strawberry Dulce de Leche Cake
- Strawberry Peanut Butter Cake

- Strawberry and Yogurt Cake
- Strawberry Pecan Praline Cake
- Strawberry-Cherry Almond Layer Cake
- Strawberry Ricotta Cake
- Strawberries and Whipped Ganache Cake
- Strawberry Custard Cake
- Strawberry Chiffon Cake
- Strawberry Coffee Layer Cake
- Strawberries and Hazelnut Cake
- Strawberry and Fig Layer Cake
- Strawberry-Coconut Meringue Cake
- Strawberry Banana Split Layer Cake
- Strawberry Lemon Poppy Seed Cake
- Strawberry Lavender Layer Cake
- Strawberry and Cashew Cream Cake

Classic Strawberry Shortcake Layer Cake

Ingredients
For the Cake:

- 2 ½ cups (315g) all-purpose flour
- 2 ½ tsp baking powder
- ½ tsp salt
- 1 cup (230g) unsalted butter, softened
- 2 cups (400g) granulated sugar
- 4 large eggs
- 2 tsp vanilla extract
- 1 cup (240ml) whole milk

For the Strawberry Filling:

- 2 cups (300g) fresh strawberries, sliced
- ¼ cup (50g) granulated sugar
- 1 tbsp lemon juice

For the Whipped Cream Frosting:

- 2 cups (480ml) heavy whipping cream, chilled
- ½ cup (60g) powdered sugar
- 1 tsp vanilla extract

Instructions

1. **Prepare the Cake Layers:**
   Preheat your oven to 350°F (175°C). Grease and flour two 9-inch round cake pans.
   In a medium bowl, sift together the flour, baking powder, and salt. Set aside.
   In a large bowl, cream the butter and sugar until light and fluffy. Add the eggs, one at a time, beating well after each addition. Stir in the vanilla extract.
   Gradually add the flour mixture, alternating with the milk, beginning and ending with the dry ingredients. Mix until just combined.
   Divide the batter evenly between the prepared pans and bake for 25–30 minutes, or until a toothpick inserted into the center comes out clean. Let the cakes cool completely on a wire rack.
2. **Make the Strawberry Filling:**
   In a medium bowl, toss the sliced strawberries with sugar and lemon juice. Let

the mixture sit for about 15–20 minutes until the strawberries release their juices.

3. **Prepare the Whipped Cream Frosting:**
   In a chilled bowl, whip the heavy cream with powdered sugar and vanilla extract until stiff peaks form. Be careful not to overbeat.

4. **Assemble the Cake:**
   Place one cake layer on a serving plate. Spread a layer of whipped cream on top, followed by a generous layer of the strawberry filling.
   Place the second cake layer on top and repeat with another layer of whipped cream and strawberries.
   Spread whipped cream around the sides and top of the cake for a smooth finish. Garnish with additional fresh strawberries if desired.

5. **Chill and Serve:**
   Refrigerate the cake for at least 1 hour before serving to allow the flavors to meld. Slice and enjoy!

Strawberries and Cream Drip Cake

Ingredients
For the Cake:

- 2 ½ cups (315g) all-purpose flour
- 2 ½ tsp baking powder
- ½ tsp salt
- 1 cup (230g) unsalted butter, softened
- 2 cups (400g) granulated sugar
- 4 large eggs
- 2 tsp vanilla extract
- 1 cup (240ml) whole milk

For the Filling and Frosting:

- 2 cups (300g) fresh strawberries, sliced
- 2 cups (480ml) heavy whipping cream
- ½ cup (60g) powdered sugar
- 1 tsp vanilla extract

For the Drip:

- 1 cup (240g) strawberry jam, slightly warmed

Instructions

1. Bake the cake layers using the same method as the **Classic Strawberry Shortcake Layer Cake** recipe above. Let cool completely.
2. Whip heavy cream, powdered sugar, and vanilla until stiff peaks form.
3. Spread whipped cream and sliced strawberries between cake layers. Frost the outside with the remaining whipped cream.
4. Drizzle warm strawberry jam along the edges to create the drip effect. Top with fresh strawberries for garnish. Chill before serving.

Strawberry Cheesecake Layer Cake

Ingredients
For the Cake Layers:

- Same as above.

For the Cheesecake Layer:

- 2 packages (16 oz/450g) cream cheese, softened
- ½ cup (100g) granulated sugar
- 2 large eggs
- 1 tsp vanilla extract

For the Topping:

- 1 ½ cups (225g) fresh strawberries, halved
- ½ cup (120g) strawberry jam

Instructions

1. Preheat oven to 325°F (160°C). Grease and line a 9-inch springform pan.
2. Beat cream cheese, sugar, eggs, and vanilla until smooth. Pour into the pan and bake for 40–45 minutes. Cool completely.
3. Assemble by layering cake, cheesecake, and more cake. Spread strawberry jam and arrange halved strawberries on top. Chill before serving.

Chocolate-Dipped Strawberry Cake

Ingredients
For the Cake:

- 1 ¾ cups (220g) all-purpose flour
- ¾ cup (75g) cocoa powder
- 2 tsp baking powder
- ½ tsp salt
- 1 cup (240ml) buttermilk
- ½ cup (120ml) vegetable oil
- 2 large eggs
- 1 tsp vanilla extract

For the Frosting:

- 2 cups (480ml) heavy whipping cream
- ½ cup (60g) powdered sugar
- ½ cup (120g) chocolate ganache

For Decoration:

- 12–15 strawberries dipped in melted chocolate

Instructions

1. Combine dry ingredients (flour, cocoa powder, baking powder, and salt) in one bowl and wet ingredients (buttermilk, oil, eggs, and vanilla) in another. Gradually mix them together.
2. Bake in two 9-inch round pans at 350°F (175°C) for 25–30 minutes. Cool completely.
3. Whip cream and powdered sugar until stiff. Frost the cake with whipped cream and drizzle chocolate ganache over the edges.
4. Decorate with chocolate-dipped strawberries. Chill before serving.

Strawberry-Raspberry Layer Cake

Ingredients

For the Cake:

- 2 ½ cups (310g) all-purpose flour
- 2 ½ tsp baking powder
- ½ tsp baking soda
- ½ tsp salt
- 1 cup (230g) unsalted butter, softened
- 2 cups (400g) granulated sugar
- 4 large eggs
- 1 tsp pure vanilla extract
- 1 cup (240ml) buttermilk
- ½ cup (120ml) strawberry puree (made from fresh or frozen strawberries)

For the Filling:

- 1 cup (240ml) heavy whipping cream
- 3 tbsp powdered sugar
- ½ tsp vanilla extract
- ¾ cup (100g) fresh raspberries
- ¾ cup (100g) fresh strawberries, sliced

For the Frosting:

- 1 cup (230g) unsalted butter, softened
- 4 cups (480g) powdered sugar
- 3 tbsp heavy cream or milk
- ½ cup (120ml) raspberry puree
- Fresh strawberries and raspberries for decoration (optional)

Instructions

Prepare the Cake Layers:

1. Preheat your oven to 350°F (175°C). Grease and line two 9-inch (23cm) round cake pans.
2. In a medium bowl, whisk together the flour, baking powder, baking soda, and salt.
3. In a large bowl, beat the butter and sugar together until light and fluffy (about 3 minutes).

4. Add the eggs one at a time, mixing well after each addition. Stir in the vanilla extract.
5. Alternate adding the dry ingredients and buttermilk to the batter, starting and ending with the dry ingredients. Mix until just combined.
6. Fold in the strawberry puree gently.
7. Divide the batter evenly between the prepared pans and bake for 25–30 minutes, or until a toothpick inserted in the center comes out clean.
8. Allow the cakes to cool in the pans for 10 minutes, then transfer them to a wire rack to cool completely.

Prepare the Filling:

1. In a chilled bowl, whip the heavy cream, powdered sugar, and vanilla extract until stiff peaks form.
2. Gently fold in the raspberries and sliced strawberries.

Prepare the Frosting:

1. Beat the butter in a large bowl until creamy.
2. Gradually add the powdered sugar, one cup at a time, mixing well after each addition.
3. Add the raspberry puree and cream, and beat until smooth and fluffy.

Assemble the Cake:

1. Place one cake layer on a serving plate. Spread a layer of the whipped cream and berry filling over it.
2. Top with the second cake layer. Frost the top and sides of the cake with the raspberry buttercream frosting.
3. Decorate with fresh strawberries and raspberries if desired.

Strawberry Coconut Cream Cake

Ingredients

For the Cake:

- 2 ½ cups (310g) all-purpose flour
- 2 ½ tsp baking powder
- ½ tsp baking soda
- ¼ tsp salt
- 1 cup (230g) unsalted butter, softened
- 1 ½ cups (300g) granulated sugar
- 4 large eggs
- 1 tsp vanilla extract
- 1 cup (240ml) coconut milk
- 1 ½ cups (180g) fresh strawberries, pureed
- 1 cup (80g) shredded coconut

For the Coconut Cream Frosting:

- 2 cups (480ml) heavy whipping cream
- ½ cup (60g) powdered sugar
- 1 cup (80g) shredded coconut (for garnish)
- Fresh strawberries for decoration

Instructions

1. **Prepare the Cake:**
    - Preheat the oven to 350°F (175°C). Grease and line two 9-inch (23cm) round cake pans.
    - In a medium bowl, whisk together flour, baking powder, baking soda, and salt.
    - In a large bowl, beat the butter and sugar until light and fluffy. Add the eggs one at a time, beating well after each addition. Stir in vanilla extract.
    - Alternate adding the dry ingredients and coconut milk, beginning and ending with the dry ingredients. Mix until combined.
    - Gently fold in the pureed strawberries and shredded coconut.
    - Divide the batter evenly between the pans and bake for 25–30 minutes or until a toothpick comes out clean.
    - Let the cakes cool completely.
2. **Prepare the Frosting:**

- Whip the heavy cream and powdered sugar until stiff peaks form.
- Once the cakes have cooled, spread a layer of frosting between the cake layers and around the sides.
- Garnish with shredded coconut and fresh strawberries.

Strawberry Lime Margarita Cake

Ingredients

For the Cake:

- 2 ½ cups (310g) all-purpose flour
- 2 ½ tsp baking powder
- ½ tsp baking soda
- ¼ tsp salt
- 1 cup (230g) unsalted butter, softened
- 1 ½ cups (300g) granulated sugar
- 4 large eggs
- 2 tsp lime zest
- ½ cup (120ml) lime juice
- ½ cup (120ml) tequila
- 1 cup (240ml) buttermilk
- 1 cup (180g) fresh strawberries, pureed

For the Margarita Frosting:

- 2 cups (480ml) heavy whipping cream
- ½ cup (60g) powdered sugar
- 2 tbsp lime juice
- 2 tbsp tequila
- Lime zest for garnish
- Sliced strawberries for decoration

Instructions

1. **Prepare the Cake:**
   - Preheat your oven to 350°F (175°C). Grease and line two 9-inch (23cm) round cake pans.
   - In a medium bowl, whisk together flour, baking powder, baking soda, and salt.
   - In a large bowl, beat the butter and sugar together until light and fluffy. Add the eggs one at a time, mixing well after each addition.
   - Stir in the lime zest, lime juice, and tequila.
   - Alternate adding the dry ingredients and buttermilk, beginning and ending with the dry ingredients. Mix until combined.
   - Fold in the strawberry puree.

- Divide the batter between the prepared pans and bake for 25–30 minutes, or until a toothpick inserted in the center comes out clean.
- Let the cakes cool completely.

2. **Prepare the Frosting:**
    - Whip the heavy cream and powdered sugar until stiff peaks form. Stir in the lime juice and tequila.
    - Frost the cooled cakes with the margarita frosting and garnish with lime zest and fresh strawberry slices.

Strawberry Rosewater Cake

Ingredients

For the Cake:

- 2 ½ cups (310g) all-purpose flour
- 2 ½ tsp baking powder
- ½ tsp baking soda
- ¼ tsp salt
- 1 cup (230g) unsalted butter, softened
- 1 ½ cups (300g) granulated sugar
- 4 large eggs
- 1 tsp vanilla extract
- ½ tsp rosewater extract
- 1 cup (240ml) buttermilk
- 1 cup (180g) fresh strawberries, pureed

For the Rosewater Frosting:

- 2 cups (480ml) heavy whipping cream
- ½ cup (60g) powdered sugar
- 1 tsp rosewater extract
- Fresh strawberries and rose petals for decoration

Instructions

1. **Prepare the Cake:**
    - Preheat your oven to 350°F (175°C). Grease and line two 9-inch (23cm) round cake pans.
    - In a medium bowl, whisk together flour, baking powder, baking soda, and salt.
    - In a large bowl, beat the butter and sugar until light and fluffy. Add the eggs one at a time, mixing well after each addition.
    - Stir in the vanilla extract and rosewater extract.
    - Alternate adding the dry ingredients and buttermilk, beginning and ending with the dry ingredients. Mix until combined.
    - Fold in the pureed strawberries.
    - Divide the batter between the prepared pans and bake for 25–30 minutes, or until a toothpick comes out clean.
    - Let the cakes cool completely.

2. **Prepare the Frosting:**
    - Whip the heavy cream and powdered sugar until stiff peaks form. Stir in the rosewater extract.
    - Frost the cooled cakes with the rosewater frosting. Garnish with fresh strawberries and rose petals.

Strawberry Oreo Layer Cake

Ingredients

For the Cake:

- 2 ½ cups (310g) all-purpose flour
- 2 ½ tsp baking powder
- ½ tsp baking soda
- ¼ tsp salt
- 1 cup (230g) unsalted butter, softened
- 1 ½ cups (300g) granulated sugar
- 4 large eggs
- 1 tsp vanilla extract
- 1 cup (240ml) buttermilk
- 1 cup (100g) crushed Oreo cookies

For the Filling:

- 1 cup (240ml) heavy whipping cream
- ½ cup (60g) powdered sugar
- 1 tsp vanilla extract
- 1 cup (100g) crushed Oreo cookies

For the Frosting:

- 2 cups (480ml) heavy whipping cream
- ½ cup (60g) powdered sugar
- 1 tsp vanilla extract

Instructions

1. **Prepare the Cake:**
    - Preheat your oven to 350°F (175°C). Grease and line two 9-inch (23cm) round cake pans.
    - In a medium bowl, whisk together flour, baking powder, baking soda, and salt.
    - In a large bowl, beat the butter and sugar until light and fluffy. Add the eggs one at a time, mixing well after each addition.
    - Stir in the vanilla extract.

- Alternate adding the dry ingredients and buttermilk, beginning and ending with the dry ingredients. Mix until just combined.
- Fold in the crushed Oreo cookies.
- Divide the batter evenly between the pans and bake for 25–30 minutes, or until a toothpick comes out clean.
- Let the cakes cool completely.

2. **Prepare the Filling:**
    - Whip the heavy cream and powdered sugar until stiff peaks form. Stir in the vanilla extract and fold in the crushed Oreos.
    - Spread the filling between the cake layers.

3. **Prepare the Frosting:**
    - Whip the heavy cream and powdered sugar until stiff peaks form. Stir in the vanilla extract.
    - Frost the top and sides of the cake with the whipped cream frosting.

Triple Strawberry Delight Cake

Ingredients

For the Cake:

- 2 ½ cups (310g) all-purpose flour
- 2 ½ tsp baking powder
- ½ tsp baking soda
- ¼ tsp salt
- 1 cup (230g) unsalted butter, softened
- 1 ½ cups (300g) granulated sugar
- 4 large eggs
- 1 tsp vanilla extract
- 1 cup (240ml) buttermilk
- 1 cup (180g) fresh strawberries, pureed

For the Filling:

- 1 cup (240ml) heavy whipping cream
- ½ cup (60g) powdered sugar
- 1 cup (100g) fresh strawberries, diced
- 1 cup (100g) fresh raspberries, diced
- 1 cup (100g) fresh blueberries, diced

For the Frosting:

- 2 cups (480ml) heavy whipping cream
- ½ cup (60g) powdered sugar
- 1 tsp vanilla extract
- Fresh strawberries for decoration

Instructions

1. **Prepare the Cake:**
    - Preheat the oven to 350°F (175°C). Grease and line two 9-inch (23cm) round cake pans.
    - In a medium bowl, whisk together flour, baking powder, baking soda, and salt.
    - In a large bowl, beat the butter and sugar until light and fluffy. Add the eggs one at a time, mixing well after each addition.

- Stir in the vanilla extract and pureed strawberries.
    - Alternate adding the dry ingredients and buttermilk, beginning and ending with the dry ingredients. Mix until just combined.
    - Divide the batter evenly between the pans and bake for 25–30 minutes, or until a toothpick comes out clean.
    - Let the cakes cool completely.
2. **Prepare the Filling:**
    - Whip the heavy cream and powdered sugar until stiff peaks form. Gently fold in the diced strawberries, raspberries, and blueberries.
3. **Prepare the Frosting:**
    - Whip the heavy cream and powdered sugar until stiff peaks form. Stir in the vanilla extract.
4. **Assemble the Cake:**
    - Place one cake layer on a serving plate and top with the filling.
    - Top with the second cake layer and frost with the whipped cream frosting.
    - Garnish with fresh strawberries.

Strawberry Brownie Cake

Ingredients

For the Cake:

- 1 ½ cups (190g) all-purpose flour
- 1 cup (200g) granulated sugar
- ¼ tsp baking soda
- ½ tsp salt
- ½ cup (115g) unsalted butter, melted
- 2 large eggs
- 1 tsp vanilla extract
- 1 cup (180g) fresh strawberries, pureed

For the Frosting:

- 1 cup (230g) unsalted butter, softened
- 3 cups (360g) powdered sugar
- 3 tbsp heavy cream
- 1 tsp vanilla extract
- Fresh strawberries for decoration

Instructions

1. **Prepare the Cake:**
    - Preheat the oven to 350°F (175°C). Grease and line an 8-inch square pan.
    - In a medium bowl, whisk together flour, sugar, baking soda, and salt.
    - In a large bowl, mix the melted butter, eggs, vanilla extract, and pureed strawberries.
    - Gradually add the dry ingredients to the wet ingredients and mix until combined.
    - Pour the batter into the prepared pan and bake for 20–25 minutes, or until a toothpick comes out clean.
    - Let the cake cool completely.
2. **Prepare the Frosting:**
    - Beat the butter until smooth, then gradually add powdered sugar, cream, and vanilla extract. Mix until smooth and fluffy.
3. **Assemble the Cake:**
    - Frost the cooled brownie cake with the frosting and garnish with fresh strawberries.

Strawberry Cream Cheese Pound Cake

Ingredients

For the Cake:

- 2 ½ cups (310g) all-purpose flour
- ½ tsp baking powder
- ¼ tsp salt
- 1 cup (230g) unsalted butter, softened
- 1 ½ cups (300g) granulated sugar
- 3 large eggs
- 1 tsp vanilla extract
- 1 cup (240g) cream cheese, softened
- 1 cup (180g) fresh strawberries, pureed

For the Frosting:

- 1 cup (230g) unsalted butter, softened
- 3 cups (360g) powdered sugar
- 3 tbsp heavy cream
- Fresh strawberries for decoration

Instructions

1. **Prepare the Cake:**
    - Preheat the oven to 350°F (175°C). Grease and line a 9x5-inch loaf pan.
    - In a medium bowl, whisk together flour, baking powder, and salt.
    - In a large bowl, beat the butter and sugar until light and fluffy. Add eggs one at a time, mixing well after each addition.
    - Stir in the vanilla extract and cream cheese, then fold in the pureed strawberries.
    - Gradually add the dry ingredients and mix until just combined.
    - Pour the batter into the prepared pan and bake for 60–70 minutes, or until a toothpick comes out clean.
    - Let the cake cool completely.
2. **Prepare the Frosting:**
    - Beat the butter, powdered sugar, and cream until smooth.
    - Frost the cooled cake and garnish with fresh strawberries.

Strawberry Funfetti Celebration Cake

Ingredients

For the Cake:

- 2 ½ cups (310g) all-purpose flour
- 2 ½ tsp baking powder
- ¼ tsp salt
- 1 cup (230g) unsalted butter, softened
- 1 ½ cups (300g) granulated sugar
- 4 large eggs
- 1 tsp vanilla extract
- 1 cup (240ml) buttermilk
- ½ cup (90g) rainbow sprinkles
- 1 cup (180g) fresh strawberries, pureed

For the Frosting:

- 2 cups (480ml) heavy whipping cream
- ½ cup (60g) powdered sugar
- 1 tsp vanilla extract
- Funfetti sprinkles for decoration

Instructions

1. **Prepare the Cake:**
    - Preheat the oven to 350°F (175°C). Grease and line two 9-inch (23cm) round cake pans.
    - In a medium bowl, whisk together flour, baking powder, and salt.
    - In a large bowl, beat the butter and sugar until light and fluffy. Add eggs one at a time, mixing well after each addition.
    - Stir in vanilla extract and pureed strawberries.
    - Alternate adding the dry ingredients and buttermilk, beginning and ending with the dry ingredients. Mix until just combined.
    - Fold in the sprinkles.
    - Divide the batter evenly between the pans and bake for 25–30 minutes, or until a toothpick comes out clean.
    - Let the cakes cool completely.
2. **Prepare the Frosting:**

- Whip the heavy cream and powdered sugar until stiff peaks form. Stir in the vanilla extract.
3. **Assemble the Cake:**
    - Place one cake layer on a serving plate and frost with the whipped cream.
    - Top with the second cake layer and frost the top and sides of the cake.
    - Garnish with funfetti sprinkles.

Strawberry Matcha Layer Cake

Ingredients

For the Cake:

- 2 ½ cups (310g) all-purpose flour
- 2 ½ tsp baking powder
- ¼ tsp salt
- 1 cup (230g) unsalted butter, softened
- 1 ½ cups (300g) granulated sugar
- 4 large eggs
- 1 tsp vanilla extract
- 1 cup (240ml) buttermilk
- 2 tbsp matcha powder
- 1 cup (180g) fresh strawberries, pureed

For the Frosting:

- 2 cups (480ml) heavy whipping cream
- ½ cup (60g) powdered sugar
- 1 tsp vanilla extract
- Fresh strawberries for decoration

Instructions

1. **Prepare the Cake:**
    - Preheat the oven to 350°F (175°C). Grease and line two 9-inch (23cm) round cake pans.
    - In a medium bowl, whisk together flour, baking powder, salt, and matcha powder.
    - In a large bowl, beat the butter and sugar until light and fluffy. Add eggs one at a time, mixing well after each addition.
    - Stir in the vanilla extract and pureed strawberries.
    - Alternate adding the dry ingredients and buttermilk, beginning and ending with the dry ingredients. Mix until just combined.
    - Divide the batter evenly between the pans and bake for 25–30 minutes, or until a toothpick comes out clean.
    - Let the cakes cool completely.
2. **Prepare the Frosting:**

    - Whip the heavy cream and powdered sugar until stiff peaks form. Stir in the vanilla extract.
3. **Assemble the Cake:**
    - Frost the cooled cake with the whipped cream frosting and garnish with fresh strawberries.

Strawberry Tiramisu Cake

Ingredients

For the Cake:

- 2 ½ cups (310g) all-purpose flour
- 2 ½ tsp baking powder
- ¼ tsp salt
- 1 cup (230g) unsalted butter, softened
- 1 ½ cups (300g) granulated sugar
- 4 large eggs
- 1 tsp vanilla extract
- 1 cup (240ml) buttermilk
- 1 cup (180g) fresh strawberries, pureed

For the Filling:

- 1 ½ cups (360ml) mascarpone cheese
- 1 ½ cups (360ml) heavy whipping cream
- ½ cup (60g) powdered sugar
- 1 cup (180g) fresh strawberries, pureed
- ¼ cup (60ml) coffee or espresso, cooled

For the Frosting:

- 2 cups (480ml) heavy whipping cream
- ½ cup (60g) powdered sugar
- 1 tsp vanilla extract
- Fresh strawberries for decoration

Instructions

1. **Prepare the Cake:**
    - Preheat the oven to 350°F (175°C). Grease and line two 9-inch (23cm) round cake pans.
    - In a medium bowl, whisk together flour, baking powder, and salt.
    - In a large bowl, beat the butter and sugar until light and fluffy. Add eggs one at a time, mixing well after each addition.
    - Stir in the vanilla extract and pureed strawberries.

- Alternate adding the dry ingredients and buttermilk, beginning and ending with the dry ingredients. Mix until just combined.
- Divide the batter evenly between the pans and bake for 25–30 minutes, or until a toothpick comes out clean.
- Let the cakes cool completely.

2. **Prepare the Filling:**
    - Whip the mascarpone cheese, heavy whipping cream, and powdered sugar until smooth. Add the pureed strawberries and mix well.
    - Soak the cooled cakes in coffee or espresso.

3. **Prepare the Frosting:**
    - Whip the heavy cream and powdered sugar until stiff peaks form. Stir in the vanilla extract.

4. **Assemble the Cake:**
    - Layer the soaked cakes with the mascarpone filling.
    - Frost the cake with the whipped cream frosting and garnish with fresh strawberries.

Strawberry Vanilla Bean Cake

Ingredients

For the Cake:

- 2 ½ cups (310g) all-purpose flour
- 2 ½ tsp baking powder
- ½ tsp salt
- 1 cup (230g) unsalted butter, softened
- 1 ½ cups (300g) granulated sugar
- 4 large eggs
- 1 vanilla bean pod, seeds scraped
- 1 cup (240ml) buttermilk
- 1 cup (180g) fresh strawberries, pureed

For the Frosting:

- 2 cups (480ml) heavy whipping cream
- ½ cup (60g) powdered sugar
- 1 vanilla bean pod, seeds scraped
- Fresh strawberries for decoration

Instructions

1. **Prepare the Cake:**
    - Preheat the oven to 350°F (175°C). Grease and line two 9-inch (23cm) round cake pans.
    - In a medium bowl, whisk together flour, baking powder, and salt.
    - In a large bowl, beat the butter and sugar until light and fluffy. Add eggs one at a time, mixing well after each addition.
    - Stir in the vanilla bean seeds and pureed strawberries.
    - Alternate adding the dry ingredients and buttermilk, beginning and ending with the dry ingredients. Mix until just combined.
    - Divide the batter evenly between the pans and bake for 25–30 minutes, or until a toothpick comes out clean.
    - Let the cakes cool completely.
2. **Prepare the Frosting:**
    - Whip the heavy cream and powdered sugar until stiff peaks form. Stir in the vanilla bean seeds.
3. **Assemble the Cake:**

    - Frost the cooled cake with the whipped cream frosting and garnish with fresh strawberries.

Dark Chocolate Strawberry Truffle Cake

Ingredients

For the Cake:

- 1 ½ cups (190g) all-purpose flour
- 1 cup (200g) granulated sugar
- ¼ tsp baking soda
- ½ tsp salt
- ½ cup (115g) unsalted butter, melted
- 2 large eggs
- 1 tsp vanilla extract
- 1 cup (180g) fresh strawberries, pureed
- ½ cup (50g) dark chocolate, melted

For the Filling:

- 1 cup (240ml) heavy whipping cream
- ¼ cup (50g) powdered sugar
- ½ cup (90g) fresh strawberries, diced

For the Frosting:

- 2 cups (480ml) heavy whipping cream
- ½ cup (60g) powdered sugar
- ½ cup (90g) dark chocolate, melted
- Fresh strawberries for decoration

Instructions

1. **Prepare the Cake:**
    - Preheat the oven to 350°F (175°C). Grease and line an 8-inch square pan.
    - In a medium bowl, whisk together flour, sugar, baking soda, and salt.
    - In a large bowl, mix the melted butter, eggs, vanilla extract, pureed strawberries, and melted chocolate.
    - Gradually add the dry ingredients to the wet ingredients and mix until combined.
    - Pour the batter into the prepared pan and bake for 20–25 minutes, or until a toothpick comes out clean.
    - Let the cake cool completely.

2. **Prepare the Filling:**
   - Whip the heavy cream and powdered sugar until stiff peaks form. Fold in the diced strawberries.
3. **Prepare the Frosting:**
   - Whip the heavy cream and powdered sugar until stiff peaks form. Fold in the melted chocolate.
4. **Assemble the Cake:**
   - Frost the cooled cake with the chocolate cream frosting and garnish with fresh strawberries.

Strawberries and Caramel Layer Cake

Ingredients

For the Cake:

- 2 ½ cups (310g) all-purpose flour
- 2 ½ tsp baking powder
- ¼ tsp salt
- 1 cup (230g) unsalted butter, softened
- 1 ½ cups (300g) granulated sugar
- 4 large eggs
- 1 tsp vanilla extract
- 1 cup (240ml) buttermilk
- 1 cup (180g) fresh strawberries, pureed

For the Caramel Sauce:

- 1 cup (200g) granulated sugar
- 6 tbsp (90g) unsalted butter
- ½ cup (120ml) heavy cream
- 1 tsp vanilla extract
- Pinch of salt

For the Frosting:

- 2 cups (480ml) heavy whipping cream
- ½ cup (60g) powdered sugar
- 1 tsp vanilla extract
- Fresh strawberries for decoration

Instructions

1. **Prepare the Cake:**
    - Preheat the oven to 350°F (175°C). Grease and line two 9-inch (23cm) round cake pans.
    - In a medium bowl, whisk together flour, baking powder, and salt.
    - In a large bowl, beat the butter and sugar until light and fluffy. Add eggs one at a time, mixing well after each addition.
    - Stir in the vanilla extract and pureed strawberries.

- Alternate adding the dry ingredients and buttermilk, beginning and ending with the dry ingredients. Mix until just combined.
- Divide the batter evenly between the pans and bake for 25–30 minutes, or until a toothpick comes out clean. Let the cakes cool completely.

2. **Prepare the Caramel Sauce:**
    - In a saucepan, melt the sugar over medium heat until golden and liquid.
    - Stir in the butter until melted, then add the cream, vanilla extract, and salt. Stir until smooth. Let the caramel cool.

3. **Prepare the Frosting:**
    - Whip the heavy cream and powdered sugar until stiff peaks form. Stir in the vanilla extract.

4. **Assemble the Cake:**
    - Place one cake layer on a serving plate and drizzle with a little caramel sauce. Frost with whipped cream.
    - Add the second cake layer, frost the top and sides, and drizzle with more caramel sauce. Garnish with fresh strawberries.

Strawberry Mint Layer Cake

Ingredients

For the Cake:

- 2 ½ cups (310g) all-purpose flour
- 2 ½ tsp baking powder
- ¼ tsp salt
- 1 cup (230g) unsalted butter, softened
- 1 ½ cups (300g) granulated sugar
- 4 large eggs
- 1 tsp vanilla extract
- 1 cup (240ml) buttermilk
- 1 cup (180g) fresh strawberries, pureed
- 2 tbsp fresh mint leaves, chopped

For the Frosting:

- 2 cups (480ml) heavy whipping cream
- ½ cup (60g) powdered sugar
- 1 tsp vanilla extract
- Fresh mint leaves and strawberries for decoration

Instructions

1. **Prepare the Cake:**
    - Preheat the oven to 350°F (175°C). Grease and line two 9-inch (23cm) round cake pans.
    - In a medium bowl, whisk together flour, baking powder, and salt.
    - In a large bowl, beat the butter and sugar until light and fluffy. Add eggs one at a time, mixing well after each addition.
    - Stir in the vanilla extract, pureed strawberries, and chopped mint leaves.
    - Alternate adding the dry ingredients and buttermilk, beginning and ending with the dry ingredients. Mix until just combined.
    - Divide the batter evenly between the pans and bake for 25–30 minutes, or until a toothpick comes out clean. Let the cakes cool completely.
2. **Prepare the Frosting:**
    - Whip the heavy cream and powdered sugar until stiff peaks form. Stir in the vanilla extract.
3. **Assemble the Cake:**

- Frost the cooled cake with the whipped cream frosting and garnish with fresh mint leaves and strawberries.

Strawberry Angel Food Layer Cake

Ingredients

For the Cake:

- 1 ½ cups (180g) cake flour
- 1 ½ cups (180g) powdered sugar
- 12 large egg whites
- 1 tsp vanilla extract
- 1 ½ tsp cream of tartar
- 1 cup (200g) granulated sugar
- ¼ tsp salt

For the Frosting:

- 2 cups (480ml) heavy whipping cream
- ½ cup (60g) powdered sugar
- 1 tsp vanilla extract
- Fresh strawberries for decoration

Instructions

1. **Prepare the Cake:**
    - Preheat the oven to 350°F (175°C). Grease and line an angel food cake pan.
    - Sift together the cake flour and powdered sugar. Set aside.
    - In a large mixing bowl, beat the egg whites with cream of tartar until soft peaks form.
    - Gradually add the granulated sugar and salt while beating until stiff peaks form.
    - Gently fold in the sifted flour and powdered sugar mixture and vanilla extract.
    - Pour the batter into the prepared pan and bake for 35–40 minutes, or until golden and a toothpick comes out clean. Let the cake cool upside down.
2. **Prepare the Frosting:**
    - Whip the heavy cream and powdered sugar until stiff peaks form. Stir in the vanilla extract.
3. **Assemble the Cake:**
    - Once the cake is cooled, remove it from the pan and frost the top with the whipped cream frosting. Garnish with fresh strawberries.

Roasted Strawberry and Honey Cake

Ingredients

For the Cake:

- 2 ½ cups (310g) all-purpose flour
- 2 ½ tsp baking powder
- ¼ tsp salt
- 1 cup (230g) unsalted butter, softened
- 1 ½ cups (300g) granulated sugar
- 4 large eggs
- 1 tsp vanilla extract
- 1 cup (240ml) buttermilk
- 1 cup (180g) fresh strawberries, roasted and pureed
- ¼ cup (60g) honey

For the Frosting:

- 2 cups (480ml) heavy whipping cream
- ½ cup (60g) powdered sugar
- 1 tsp vanilla extract
- Fresh strawberries for decoration

Instructions

1. **Prepare the Roasted Strawberries:**
    - Preheat the oven to 400°F (200°C). Place fresh strawberries on a baking sheet, drizzle with honey, and roast for 15–20 minutes until soft and caramelized. Puree the roasted strawberries.
2. **Prepare the Cake:**
    - Preheat the oven to 350°F (175°C). Grease and line two 9-inch (23cm) round cake pans.
    - In a medium bowl, whisk together flour, baking powder, and salt.
    - In a large bowl, beat the butter and sugar until light and fluffy. Add eggs one at a time, mixing well after each addition.
    - Stir in the vanilla extract, roasted strawberry puree, and honey.
    - Alternate adding the dry ingredients and buttermilk, beginning and ending with the dry ingredients. Mix until just combined.
    - Divide the batter evenly between the pans and bake for 25–30 minutes, or until a toothpick comes out clean. Let the cakes cool completely.

3. **Prepare the Frosting:**
    - Whip the heavy cream and powdered sugar until stiff peaks form. Stir in the vanilla extract.
4. **Assemble the Cake:**
    - Frost the cooled cake with the whipped cream frosting and garnish with fresh strawberries.

Strawberry and Pistachio Layer Cake

Ingredients

For the Cake:

- 2 ½ cups (310g) all-purpose flour
- 2 ½ tsp baking powder
- ¼ tsp salt
- 1 cup (230g) unsalted butter, softened
- 1 ½ cups (300g) granulated sugar
- 4 large eggs
- 1 tsp vanilla extract
- 1 cup (240ml) buttermilk
- 1 cup (180g) fresh strawberries, pureed
- ½ cup (60g) ground pistachios

For the Frosting:

- 2 cups (480ml) heavy whipping cream
- ½ cup (60g) powdered sugar
- 1 tsp vanilla extract
- Chopped pistachios and fresh strawberries for decoration

Instructions

1. **Prepare the Cake:**
    - Preheat the oven to 350°F (175°C). Grease and line two 9-inch (23cm) round cake pans.
    - In a medium bowl, whisk together flour, baking powder, salt, and ground pistachios.
    - In a large bowl, beat the butter and sugar until light and fluffy. Add eggs one at a time, mixing well after each addition.
    - Stir in the vanilla extract and pureed strawberries.
    - Alternate adding the dry ingredients and buttermilk, beginning and ending with the dry ingredients. Mix until just combined.
    - Divide the batter evenly between the pans and bake for 25–30 minutes, or until a toothpick comes out clean. Let the cakes cool completely.
2. **Prepare the Frosting:**
    - Whip the heavy cream and powdered sugar until stiff peaks form. Stir in the vanilla extract.

3. **Assemble the Cake:**
    - Frost the cooled cake with the whipped cream frosting and garnish with chopped pistachios and fresh strawberries.

Strawberry Cream Mille Crepe Cake

Ingredients

For the Crepes:

- 2 cups (250g) all-purpose flour
- 4 large eggs
- 1 ½ cups (360ml) milk
- ¼ cup (60g) unsalted butter, melted
- 1 tbsp vanilla extract
- 1 tbsp sugar

For the Filling:

- 2 cups (480ml) heavy whipping cream
- ½ cup (60g) powdered sugar
- 1 tsp vanilla extract
- Fresh strawberries for decoration

Instructions

1. **Prepare the Crepes:**
   - In a bowl, whisk together flour, eggs, milk, melted butter, vanilla extract, and sugar until smooth.
   - Heat a non-stick pan over medium heat and lightly grease. Pour in a small amount of batter, swirling to cover the bottom. Cook for 1–2 minutes on each side. Repeat until all crepes are cooked.
2. **Prepare the Filling:**
   - Whip the heavy cream and powdered sugar until stiff peaks form. Stir in the vanilla extract.
3. **Assemble the Cake:**
   - Layer crepes with the whipped cream filling between each layer. Repeat the layers until all crepes are stacked. Frost the top layer with more whipped cream and garnish with fresh strawberries.

Strawberry Champagne Cake

Ingredients

For the Cake:

- 2 ½ cups (310g) all-purpose flour
- 2 ½ tsp baking powder
- ¼ tsp salt
- 1 cup (230g) unsalted butter, softened
- 1 ½ cups (300g) granulated sugar
- 4 large eggs
- 1 tsp vanilla extract
- ¾ cup (180ml) champagne
- 1 cup (180g) fresh strawberries, pureed

For the Frosting:

- 2 cups (480ml) heavy whipping cream
- ½ cup (60g) powdered sugar
- 1 tsp vanilla extract
- Fresh strawberries for decoration

Instructions

1. **Prepare the Cake:**
    - Preheat the oven to 350°F (175°C). Grease and line two 9-inch (23cm) round cake pans.
    - In a medium bowl, whisk together flour, baking powder, and salt.
    - In a large bowl, beat the butter and sugar until light and fluffy. Add eggs one at a time, mixing well after each addition.
    - Stir in the vanilla extract, champagne, and pureed strawberries.
    - Alternate adding the dry ingredients and wet ingredients, beginning and ending with the dry ingredients. Mix until just combined.
    - Divide the batter evenly between the pans and bake for 25–30 minutes, or until a toothpick comes out clean. Let the cakes cool completely.
2. **Prepare the Frosting:**
    - Whip the heavy cream and powdered sugar until stiff peaks form. Stir in the vanilla extract.
3. **Assemble the Cake:**

- Frost the cooled cake with the whipped cream frosting and garnish with fresh strawberries.

Strawberry Dulce de Leche Cake

Ingredients

For the Cake:

- 2 ½ cups (310g) all-purpose flour
- 2 ½ tsp baking powder
- ¼ tsp salt
- 1 cup (230g) unsalted butter, softened
- 1 ½ cups (300g) granulated sugar
- 4 large eggs
- 1 tsp vanilla extract
- ½ cup (120ml) dulce de leche
- 1 cup (180g) fresh strawberries, pureed

For the Frosting:

- 2 cups (480ml) heavy whipping cream
- ½ cup (60g) powdered sugar
- 1 tsp vanilla extract
- Dulce de leche for drizzling

Instructions

1. **Prepare the Cake:**
    - Preheat the oven to 350°F (175°C). Grease and line two 9-inch (23cm) round cake pans.
    - In a medium bowl, whisk together flour, baking powder, and salt.
    - In a large bowl, beat the butter and sugar until light and fluffy. Add eggs one at a time, mixing well after each addition.
    - Stir in the vanilla extract, dulce de leche, and pureed strawberries.
    - Alternate adding the dry ingredients and wet ingredients, beginning and ending with the dry ingredients. Mix until just combined.
    - Divide the batter evenly between the pans and bake for 25–30 minutes, or until a toothpick comes out clean. Let the cakes cool completely.
2. **Prepare the Frosting:**
    - Whip the heavy cream and powdered sugar until stiff peaks form. Stir in the vanilla extract.
3. **Assemble the Cake:**

- Frost the cooled cake with the whipped cream frosting, drizzle with dulce de leche, and garnish with fresh strawberries.

Strawberry Peanut Butter Cake

Ingredients

For the Cake:

- 2 ½ cups (310g) all-purpose flour
- 2 tsp baking powder
- ½ tsp baking soda
- ¼ tsp salt
- 1 cup (230g) unsalted butter, softened
- 1 cup (250g) peanut butter
- 1 ½ cups (300g) granulated sugar
- 3 large eggs
- 1 tsp vanilla extract
- 1 cup (240ml) buttermilk
- 1 cup (180g) fresh strawberries, pureed

For the Frosting:

- 1 cup (230g) peanut butter
- 2 cups (480ml) heavy whipping cream
- ½ cup (60g) powdered sugar
- 1 tsp vanilla extract

Instructions

1. **Prepare the Cake:**
   - Preheat the oven to 350°F (175°C). Grease and line two 9-inch (23cm) round cake pans.
   - In a bowl, whisk together flour, baking powder, baking soda, and salt.
   - In a large bowl, beat together butter, peanut butter, and sugar until fluffy. Add eggs one at a time, mixing well after each addition. Stir in vanilla extract.
   - Gradually add the dry ingredients, alternating with buttermilk. Stir in the pureed strawberries.
   - Divide the batter between the pans and bake for 25–30 minutes or until a toothpick comes out clean. Let the cakes cool completely.
2. **Prepare the Frosting:**
   - Beat the peanut butter, heavy cream, powdered sugar, and vanilla until smooth and fluffy.

3. **Assemble the Cake:**
    - Frost the cooled cake with the peanut butter frosting. Garnish with chopped peanuts or additional strawberries.

Strawberry and Yogurt Cake

Ingredients

For the Cake:

- 2 ½ cups (310g) all-purpose flour
- 1 ½ tsp baking powder
- ½ tsp baking soda
- ¼ tsp salt
- 1 cup (230g) unsalted butter, softened
- 1 cup (200g) granulated sugar
- 3 large eggs
- 1 tsp vanilla extract
- 1 cup (240g) plain yogurt
- 1 cup (180g) fresh strawberries, pureed

For the Frosting:

- 2 cups (480ml) heavy whipping cream
- ½ cup (60g) powdered sugar
- 1 tsp vanilla extract
- Fresh strawberries for decoration

Instructions

1. **Prepare the Cake:**
    - Preheat the oven to 350°F (175°C). Grease and line two 9-inch (23cm) round cake pans.
    - In a bowl, whisk together flour, baking powder, baking soda, and salt.
    - In a large bowl, beat the butter and sugar until light and fluffy. Add eggs one at a time, mixing well after each addition. Stir in vanilla extract.
    - Add the yogurt and pureed strawberries, mixing until combined. Gradually add the dry ingredients and mix until just combined.
    - Divide the batter between the pans and bake for 25–30 minutes or until a toothpick comes out clean. Let the cakes cool completely.
2. **Prepare the Frosting:**
    - Whip the heavy cream and powdered sugar until stiff peaks form. Stir in vanilla extract.
3. **Assemble the Cake:**

- Frost the cooled cake with whipped cream and decorate with fresh strawberries.

Strawberry Pecan Praline Cake

Ingredients

For the Cake:

- 2 ½ cups (310g) all-purpose flour
- 2 tsp baking powder
- ½ tsp baking soda
- ¼ tsp salt
- 1 cup (230g) unsalted butter, softened
- 1 ½ cups (300g) brown sugar
- 3 large eggs
- 1 tsp vanilla extract
- 1 cup (240ml) buttermilk
- 1 cup (180g) fresh strawberries, chopped
- ½ cup (60g) chopped pecans

For the Frosting:

- 2 cups (480ml) heavy whipping cream
- ½ cup (60g) powdered sugar
- 1 tsp vanilla extract
- ½ cup (60g) chopped pecans, toasted
- ½ cup (120g) praline syrup

Instructions

1. **Prepare the Cake:**
    - Preheat the oven to 350°F (175°C). Grease and line two 9-inch (23cm) round cake pans.
    - In a bowl, whisk together flour, baking powder, baking soda, and salt.
    - In a large bowl, beat the butter and brown sugar until fluffy. Add eggs one at a time, mixing well after each addition. Stir in vanilla extract.
    - Add the buttermilk and gradually add the dry ingredients, mixing until just combined. Fold in the chopped strawberries and chopped pecans.
    - Divide the batter between the pans and bake for 25–30 minutes or until a toothpick comes out clean. Let the cakes cool completely.
2. **Prepare the Frosting:**
    - Whip the heavy cream and powdered sugar until stiff peaks form. Stir in vanilla extract.

		- Gently fold in the toasted pecans and praline syrup.
3. **Assemble the Cake:**
	- Frost the cooled cake with the whipped cream mixture and garnish with additional pecans and praline syrup.

Strawberry-Cherry Almond Layer Cake

Ingredients

For the Cake:

- 2 ½ cups (310g) all-purpose flour
- 1 ½ tsp baking powder
- ¼ tsp salt
- 1 cup (230g) unsalted butter, softened
- 1 ½ cups (300g) granulated sugar
- 3 large eggs
- 1 tsp almond extract
- 1 cup (240ml) milk
- 1 cup (180g) fresh strawberries, chopped
- ½ cup (80g) fresh cherries, chopped

For the Frosting:

- 2 cups (480ml) heavy whipping cream
- ½ cup (60g) powdered sugar
- 1 tsp vanilla extract
- Fresh strawberries and cherries for decoration

Instructions

1. **Prepare the Cake:**
    - Preheat the oven to 350°F (175°C). Grease and line two 9-inch (23cm) round cake pans.
    - In a bowl, whisk together flour, baking powder, and salt.
    - In a large bowl, beat the butter and sugar until light and fluffy. Add eggs one at a time, mixing well after each addition. Stir in almond extract.
    - Gradually add the dry ingredients alternating with milk. Stir in the chopped strawberries and cherries.
    - Divide the batter between the pans and bake for 25–30 minutes or until a toothpick comes out clean. Let the cakes cool completely.
2. **Prepare the Frosting:**
    - Whip the heavy cream and powdered sugar until stiff peaks form. Stir in vanilla extract.
3. **Assemble the Cake:**

- Frost the cooled cake with whipped cream and decorate with fresh strawberries and cherries.

Strawberry Ricotta Cake

Ingredients

For the Cake:

- 2 ½ cups (310g) all-purpose flour
- 1 ½ tsp baking powder
- ½ tsp salt
- 1 cup (230g) unsalted butter, softened
- 1 ½ cups (300g) granulated sugar
- 3 large eggs
- 1 cup (240g) ricotta cheese
- 1 tsp vanilla extract
- 1 cup (180g) fresh strawberries, pureed

For the Frosting:

- 1 cup (230g) ricotta cheese
- 2 cups (480ml) heavy whipping cream
- ½ cup (60g) powdered sugar
- 1 tsp vanilla extract
- Fresh strawberries for decoration

Instructions

1. **Prepare the Cake:**
    - Preheat the oven to 350°F (175°C). Grease and line two 9-inch (23cm) round cake pans.
    - In a bowl, whisk together flour, baking powder, and salt.
    - In a large bowl, beat the butter and sugar until light and fluffy. Add eggs one at a time, mixing well after each addition. Stir in ricotta cheese and vanilla extract.
    - Gradually add the dry ingredients and fold in pureed strawberries.
    - Divide the batter between the pans and bake for 25–30 minutes or until a toothpick comes out clean. Let the cakes cool completely.
2. **Prepare the Frosting:**
    - Beat the ricotta cheese, heavy cream, powdered sugar, and vanilla until smooth and fluffy.
3. **Assemble the Cake:**

- Frost the cooled cake with ricotta frosting and decorate with fresh strawberries.

Strawberries and Whipped Ganache Cake

Ingredients

For the Cake:

- 2 ½ cups (310g) all-purpose flour
- 1 ½ tsp baking powder
- ½ tsp salt
- 1 cup (230g) unsalted butter, softened
- 1 ½ cups (300g) granulated sugar
- 3 large eggs
- 1 tsp vanilla extract
- 1 cup (240ml) milk
- 1 cup (180g) fresh strawberries, chopped

For the Frosting:

- 1 cup (240g) heavy whipping cream
- 8 oz (225g) dark chocolate, chopped
- 1 tsp vanilla extract
- Fresh strawberries for decoration

Instructions

1. **Prepare the Cake:**
    - Preheat the oven to 350°F (175°C). Grease and line two 9-inch (23cm) round cake pans.
    - In a bowl, whisk together flour, baking powder, and salt.
    - In a large bowl, beat the butter and sugar until light and fluffy. Add eggs one at a time, mixing well after each addition. Stir in vanilla extract.
    - Gradually add the dry ingredients alternating with milk. Fold in the chopped strawberries.
    - Divide the batter between the pans and bake for 25–30 minutes or until a toothpick comes out clean. Let the cakes cool completely.
2. **Prepare the Frosting:**
    - Heat the heavy cream in a saucepan until just about to boil. Pour over the chopped dark chocolate and stir until smooth. Stir in vanilla extract and let the ganache cool.
    - Whip the cooled ganache until light and fluffy.
3. **Assemble the Cake:**

- Frost the cooled cake with whipped ganache and decorate with fresh strawberries.

Strawberry Custard Cake

Ingredients

For the Cake:

- 2 ½ cups (310g) all-purpose flour
- 1 ½ tsp baking powder
- ¼ tsp salt
- 1 cup (230g) unsalted butter, softened
- 1 ½ cups (300g) granulated sugar
- 3 large eggs
- 1 tsp vanilla extract
- 1 cup (240ml) milk
- 1 cup (180g) fresh strawberries, pureed

For the Custard:

- 1 cup (240ml) whole milk
- 3 large egg yolks
- ½ cup (100g) sugar
- 1 tsp vanilla extract

Instructions

1. **Prepare the Cake:**
    - Preheat the oven to 350°F (175°C). Grease and line two 9-inch (23cm) round cake pans.
    - In a bowl, whisk together flour, baking powder, and salt.
    - In a large bowl, beat the butter and sugar until light and fluffy. Add eggs one at a time, mixing well after each addition. Stir in vanilla extract.
    - Gradually add the dry ingredients alternating with milk. Fold in pureed strawberries.
    - Divide the batter between the pans and bake for 25–30 minutes or until a toothpick comes out clean. Let the cakes cool completely.
2. **Prepare the Custard:**
    - Heat the milk in a saucepan until just about to boil. Whisk egg yolks with sugar and pour the hot milk over the yolks while whisking constantly.
    - Return the mixture to the pan and cook over medium heat until thickened. Stir in vanilla extract and cool completely.
3. **Assemble the Cake:**

    - Frost the cooled cake with custard and garnish with fresh strawberries.

Strawberry Chiffon Cake

Ingredients

For the Cake:

- 2 ½ cups (310g) all-purpose flour
- 1 ½ tsp baking powder
- ¼ tsp salt
- 1 cup (230g) unsalted butter, softened
- 1 ½ cups (300g) granulated sugar
- 3 large eggs
- 1 tsp vanilla extract
- 1 cup (240ml) milk
- 1 cup (180g) fresh strawberries, pureed

For the Frosting:

- 2 cups (480ml) heavy whipping cream
- ½ cup (60g) powdered sugar
- 1 tsp vanilla extract

Instructions

1. **Prepare the Cake:**
    - Preheat the oven to 350°F (175°C). Grease and line two 9-inch (23cm) round cake pans.
    - In a bowl, whisk together flour, baking powder, and salt.
    - In a large bowl, beat the butter and sugar until light and fluffy. Add eggs one at a time, mixing well after each addition. Stir in vanilla extract.
    - Gradually add the dry ingredients alternating with milk. Fold in pureed strawberries.
    - Divide the batter between the pans and bake for 25–30 minutes or until a toothpick comes out clean. Let the cakes cool completely.
2. **Prepare the Frosting:**
    - Whip the heavy cream and powdered sugar until stiff peaks form. Stir in vanilla extract.
3. **Assemble the Cake:**
    - Frost the cooled cake with whipped cream and decorate with fresh strawberries.

Strawberry Coffee Layer Cake

Ingredients

For the Cake:

- 2 ½ cups (310g) all-purpose flour
- 2 tsp baking powder
- ½ tsp salt
- 1 cup (230g) unsalted butter, softened
- 1 ½ cups (300g) granulated sugar
- 3 large eggs
- 1 tsp vanilla extract
- 1 cup (240ml) brewed coffee
- 1 cup (180g) fresh strawberries, chopped

For the Frosting:

- 2 cups (480ml) heavy whipping cream
- ½ cup (60g) powdered sugar
- 1 tsp vanilla extract
- Fresh strawberries for decoration

Instructions

1. **Prepare the Cake:**
    - Preheat the oven to 350°F (175°C). Grease and line two 9-inch (23cm) round cake pans.
    - In a bowl, whisk together flour, baking powder, and salt.
    - In a large bowl, beat the butter and sugar until light and fluffy. Add eggs one at a time, mixing well after each addition. Stir in vanilla extract.
    - Gradually add the dry ingredients alternating with brewed coffee. Stir in chopped strawberries.
    - Divide the batter between the pans and bake for 25–30 minutes or until a toothpick comes out clean. Let the cakes cool completely.
2. **Prepare the Frosting:**
    - Whip the heavy cream and powdered sugar until stiff peaks form. Stir in vanilla extract.
3. **Assemble the Cake:**
    - Frost the cooled cake with whipped cream and decorate with fresh strawberries.

Strawberries and Hazelnut Cake

Ingredients

For the Cake:

- 2 ½ cups (310g) all-purpose flour
- 1 ½ tsp baking powder
- ¼ tsp salt
- 1 cup (230g) unsalted butter, softened
- 1 ½ cups (300g) granulated sugar
- 3 large eggs
- 1 tsp vanilla extract
- 1 cup (240ml) milk
- 1 cup (180g) fresh strawberries, chopped
- ½ cup (60g) roasted hazelnuts, chopped

For the Frosting:

- 1 cup (240ml) heavy whipping cream
- 8 oz (225g) dark chocolate, chopped
- 1 tsp vanilla extract
- Crushed hazelnuts for decoration

Instructions

1. **Prepare the Cake:**
    - Preheat the oven to 350°F (175°C). Grease and line two 9-inch (23cm) round cake pans.
    - In a bowl, whisk together flour, baking powder, and salt.
    - In a large bowl, beat the butter and sugar until light and fluffy. Add eggs one at a time, mixing well after each addition. Stir in vanilla extract.
    - Gradually add the dry ingredients alternating with milk. Fold in chopped strawberries and roasted hazelnuts.
    - Divide the batter between the pans and bake for 25–30 minutes or until a toothpick comes out clean. Let the cakes cool completely.
2. **Prepare the Frosting:**
    - Heat the heavy cream in a saucepan until just about to boil. Pour over the chopped dark chocolate and stir until smooth. Stir in vanilla extract and let the ganache cool.
    - Whip the cooled ganache until light and fluffy.

3. **Assemble the Cake:**
    - Frost the cooled cake with whipped ganache and decorate with crushed hazelnuts.

Strawberry and Fig Layer Cake

Ingredients

For the Cake:

- 2 ½ cups (310g) all-purpose flour
- 1 ½ tsp baking powder
- ¼ tsp salt
- 1 cup (230g) unsalted butter, softened
- 1 ½ cups (300g) granulated sugar
- 3 large eggs
- 1 tsp vanilla extract
- 1 cup (240ml) milk
- 1 cup (180g) fresh strawberries, chopped
- 1 cup (150g) dried figs, chopped

For the Frosting:

- 1 ½ cups (360ml) heavy whipping cream
- 8 oz (225g) cream cheese, softened
- ½ cup (60g) powdered sugar
- Fresh figs for decoration

Instructions

1. **Prepare the Cake:**
    - Preheat the oven to 350°F (175°C). Grease and line two 9-inch (23cm) round cake pans.
    - In a bowl, whisk together flour, baking powder, and salt.
    - In a large bowl, beat the butter and sugar until light and fluffy. Add eggs one at a time, mixing well after each addition. Stir in vanilla extract.
    - Gradually add the dry ingredients alternating with milk. Fold in chopped strawberries and figs.
    - Divide the batter between the pans and bake for 25–30 minutes or until a toothpick comes out clean. Let the cakes cool completely.
2. **Prepare the Frosting:**
    - In a bowl, beat the cream cheese until smooth. Add powdered sugar and whipping cream, and beat until fluffy.
3. **Assemble the Cake:**

    - Frost the cooled cake with cream cheese frosting and decorate with fresh figs.

Strawberry-Coconut Meringue Cake

Ingredients

For the Cake:

- 2 ½ cups (310g) all-purpose flour
- 1 ½ tsp baking powder
- ¼ tsp salt
- 1 cup (230g) unsalted butter, softened
- 1 ½ cups (300g) granulated sugar
- 3 large eggs
- 1 tsp vanilla extract
- 1 cup (240ml) milk
- 1 cup (180g) fresh strawberries, chopped
- 1 cup (100g) shredded coconut

For the Meringue:

- 4 large egg whites
- 1 cup (200g) granulated sugar
- ½ tsp vanilla extract

For the Frosting:

- 1 cup (240ml) heavy whipping cream
- ½ cup (50g) shredded coconut, toasted

Instructions

1. **Prepare the Cake:**
    - Preheat the oven to 350°F (175°C). Grease and line two 9-inch (23cm) round cake pans.
    - In a bowl, whisk together flour, baking powder, and salt.
    - In a large bowl, beat the butter and sugar until light and fluffy. Add eggs one at a time, mixing well after each addition. Stir in vanilla extract.
    - Gradually add the dry ingredients alternating with milk. Fold in chopped strawberries and shredded coconut.
    - Divide the batter between the pans and bake for 25–30 minutes or until a toothpick comes out clean. Let the cakes cool completely.
2. **Prepare the Meringue:**

- Beat egg whites with sugar until stiff peaks form. Stir in vanilla extract.
    - Spread meringue over the cooled cakes and bake at 325°F (160°C) for 10–15 minutes or until golden.
3. **Prepare the Frosting:**
    - Whip the heavy cream until stiff peaks form.
4. **Assemble the Cake:**
    - Frost the cooled cake with whipped cream and top with toasted coconut.

Strawberry Banana Split Layer Cake

Ingredients

For the Cake:

- 2 ½ cups (310g) all-purpose flour
- 1 ½ tsp baking powder
- ¼ tsp salt
- 1 cup (230g) unsalted butter, softened
- 1 ½ cups (300g) granulated sugar
- 3 large eggs
- 1 tsp vanilla extract
- 1 cup (240ml) milk
- 1 cup (180g) fresh strawberries, chopped
- 1 ripe banana, mashed

For the Frosting:

- 2 cups (480ml) heavy whipping cream
- ½ cup (60g) powdered sugar
- ½ cup (100g) chocolate syrup
- Fresh strawberries, banana slices, and maraschino cherries for decoration

Instructions

1. **Prepare the Cake:**
    - Preheat the oven to 350°F (175°C). Grease and line two 9-inch (23cm) round cake pans.
    - In a bowl, whisk together flour, baking powder, and salt.
    - In a large bowl, beat the butter and sugar until light and fluffy. Add eggs one at a time, mixing well after each addition. Stir in vanilla extract.
    - Gradually add the dry ingredients alternating with milk. Fold in chopped strawberries and mashed banana.
    - Divide the batter between the pans and bake for 25–30 minutes or until a toothpick comes out clean. Let the cakes cool completely.
2. **Prepare the Frosting:**
    - Whip the heavy cream with powdered sugar until stiff peaks form.
    - Fold in chocolate syrup.
3. **Assemble the Cake:**

- Frost the cooled cake with whipped cream and decorate with strawberry slices, banana slices, and maraschino cherries.

Strawberry Lemon Poppy Seed Cake

Ingredients

For the Cake:

- 2 ½ cups (310g) all-purpose flour
- 1 ½ tsp baking powder
- ¼ tsp salt
- 1 cup (230g) unsalted butter, softened
- 1 ½ cups (300g) granulated sugar
- 3 large eggs
- 1 tsp vanilla extract
- 1 cup (240ml) milk
- 1 cup (180g) fresh strawberries, chopped
- 2 tbsp poppy seeds
- Zest of 1 lemon

For the Frosting:

- 2 cups (480ml) heavy whipping cream
- 1 tbsp lemon zest
- ½ cup (60g) powdered sugar

Instructions

1. **Prepare the Cake:**
    - Preheat the oven to 350°F (175°C). Grease and line two 9-inch (23cm) round cake pans.
    - In a bowl, whisk together flour, baking powder, salt, poppy seeds, and lemon zest.
    - In a large bowl, beat the butter and sugar until light and fluffy. Add eggs one at a time, mixing well after each addition. Stir in vanilla extract.
    - Gradually add the dry ingredients alternating with milk. Fold in chopped strawberries.
    - Divide the batter between the pans and bake for 25–30 minutes or until a toothpick comes out clean. Let the cakes cool completely.
2. **Prepare the Frosting:**
    - Whip the heavy cream with powdered sugar and lemon zest until stiff peaks form.
3. **Assemble the Cake:**

    - Frost the cooled cake with lemon whipped cream and decorate with extra lemon zest and strawberries.

Strawberry Lavender Layer Cake

Ingredients

For the Cake:

- 2 ½ cups (310g) all-purpose flour
- 1 ½ tsp baking powder
- ¼ tsp salt
- 1 cup (230g) unsalted butter, softened
- 1 ½ cups (300g) granulated sugar
- 3 large eggs
- 1 tsp vanilla extract
- 1 cup (240ml) milk
- 1 cup (180g) fresh strawberries, chopped
- 1 tbsp culinary lavender, finely chopped

For the Frosting:

- 2 cups (480ml) heavy whipping cream
- 2 tbsp powdered sugar
- 1 tsp vanilla extract
- Dried lavender for decoration

Instructions

1. **Prepare the Cake:**
   - Preheat the oven to 350°F (175°C). Grease and line two 9-inch (23cm) round cake pans.
   - In a bowl, whisk together flour, baking powder, salt, and lavender.
   - In a large bowl, beat the butter and sugar until light and fluffy. Add eggs one at a time, mixing well after each addition. Stir in vanilla extract.
   - Gradually add the dry ingredients alternating with milk. Fold in chopped strawberries.
   - Divide the batter between the pans and bake for 25–30 minutes or until a toothpick comes out clean. Let the cakes cool completely.
2. **Prepare the Frosting:**
   - Whip the heavy cream with powdered sugar and vanilla extract until stiff peaks form.
3. **Assemble the Cake:**

- Frost the cooled cake with lavender-infused whipped cream and decorate with dried lavender.

www.ingramcontent.com/pod-product-compliance
Lightning Source LLC
LaVergne TN
LVHW081618060526
838201LV00054B/2295